*Take the power
to make your life
healthy
exciting
worthwhile
and very happy*

~ Susan Polis Schutz

Other books in this series...

Blue Mountain Arts®

A Friend Lives in Your Heart Forever

A Mother Is Love

I Love You Soooo Much
by Douglas Pagels

I'd Love to Give These Gifts to You

Keep Believing in Yourself and Your Special Dreams

Sister, You Have a Special Place in My Heart

The Greatest Gift of All Is... A Daughter like You

The Greatest Gift of All Is... A Son like You

Promises to Myself

A Blue Mountain Arts® Collection
to Help You Create the Life
You've Always Dreamed Of

Edited by Suzanne Moore

SPS Studios™
Boulder, Colorado

Library of Congress Control Number: 2002095117
ISBN: 0-88396-714-6

The introductions to each section in this book were written by Suzanne Moore and Douglas Pagels, with the exception of "Promise Yourself to Be a Better Friend" by Emilienne Motaze and "Promise Yourself to Live Each Day with Love" by Barbara Cage.

We wish to thank Susan Polis Schutz for permission to reprint the following poem that appears in this publication: "This life is yours." Copyright © 1978 by Continental Publications. All rights reserved.

ACKNOWLEDGMENTS appear on page 48.

Certain trademarks are used under license.

Manufactured in Thailand.
First Printing: 2003

 This book is printed on recycled paper.

SPS Studios, Inc.

P.O. Box 4549, Boulder, Colorado 80306

Contents

———— ❧ ————

Promise Yourself to...

Destiny is not a matter of chance,
it is a matter of choice;
it is not a thing to be waited for,
it is a thing to be achieved.

~ William J. Bryan

Introduction

We all have things we wish we could change about our lives. We all have times when we feel frustrated with what we've been given ~ moments when we find ourselves wishing for more. It's easy to sit back and wait for your life to change, relying on chance to bring good things your way. But dreams don't come true by themselves, and the things you're wishing for will not just appear. There comes a time when you have to recognize that life is not something that just happens to you. It's up to you to design it. The most enlightening realization is also the scariest. It is the instant when you begin to understand that your life can be whatever you want it to be.

Starting today, embrace that realization. Instead of settling for a life that isn't all it could be, promise yourself to reach out for more. Promise yourself to be all the things you always wished you could be. Promise yourself to seek out whatever you need to be happy. If you aren't sure where to begin, promise yourself not to wait another moment before trying to find out. This life is the only one you're given ~ above all, promise yourself to make it one worth remembering.

Promise Yourself to...

Be the Person
You Always Wanted to Be

———————— ✾ ————————

Starting today, I will be the best person I can be. I won't wait until the beginning of the year to make resolutions. I will realize that each day is a new beginning. Every day, I'm given the chance to open my eyes, put my feet on the ground, and take one more step toward becoming the person I want to be. Instead of dreaming, I will set goals. Instead of imagining, I will take steps. Instead of saying "one day," I will say "starting today."

———————— ✾ ————————

It is never too late to be
what you might have been.

~ George Eliot

Imagine yourself to be the type of person you want to be, and then be it. You may have to let go of some bad habits and develop some more positive ones, but don't give up ~ for it is only through trying and persisting that dreams come true.

Expect changes to occur, and realize that the power to make those changes comes from within you. Your thoughts and actions, your choices and decisions, and the way you spend your time determine who you are and who you will become.

You are capable and worthy of being and doing anything. You just need the discipline and determination to see it through. It won't come instantly, and you may backslide from time to time, but don't let that deter you. Never give up.

Life is an ever-changing process, and nothing is final. Therefore, each moment and every day is a chance to begin anew.

~ Barbara Cage

Promise Yourself to...

Believe in Yourself

———— ❦ ————

I will remember that I can do anything I set my mind to. I can achieve any goal, fulfill any desire, and reach any star. I will look toward tomorrow with the conviction that I can make it better. I will know that a brighter future is within my reach... as long as I have the strength to keep trying, the courage to keep striving, and the confidence to keep believing in myself.

———— ❦ ————

As you go on in this world, keep looking forward to the future... to all you might be. As far as who you are and who you will become goes ~ the answer is always within yourself. Believe in yourself. Follow your heart and your dreams. You ~ like everyone else ~ will make mistakes. But as long as you are true to the strength within your own heart... you can never go wrong.

~ Ashley Rice

Having faith in yourself is what makes it possible to have the determination to see things through. You control your destiny, and having faith in yourself controls how far you can go.

Knowing in your heart that you are in charge can give you the power to overcome obstacles. It's an attitude that carries you through the tough times and that looks at the positives and defies the negatives.

Nothing worthwhile comes easily, and only you can decide the sacrifices, the effort, and the passion you're willing to put into the different parts of your life.

Look into your heart, search your dreams, and be honest about what you really want; then do whatever it takes to get it.

Live like you mean it. Believe you can... and you will!

~ Barbara Cage

Be Proud of Who You Are

———— ❦ ————

I am not perfect,
but I am perfectly me.
I will improve the things I can change
and accept the things I can't.
I will forgive myself when I fail
and congratulate myself when I succeed.
I will know that my best is always enough.
I will believe in myself
and do all I can to reach my dreams.
I will look in the mirror
and see a friend.
I will be kind to myself,
love myself, and
celebrate myself
each day and every moment.

———— ❦ ————

When you look in the mirror in the days ahead, may you smile a hundred times more than you frown at what you see. Smile because you know that a loving, capable, sensible, strong, precious person is reflected there.

~ Laurel Atherton

Feel really good about who you are.
Appreciate your uniqueness.
Acknowledge your talents and abilities.
Realize what a beautiful soul you have.
Understand the wonder within.

~ Sydney Nealson

Love and respect everything that
you are and will become.
Reap the fruits of your talents, and
walk with pride down the road of life.

~ Jackie Olson

Promise Yourself to...

Live Your Life to Its Fullest

———— ❧ ————

This life is the only one I'm given. I will live it well. I will do all I can to make the most of each day, each minute, and each moment. I will never say the words "I wish," "what if," or "maybe someday." I will do the things I've always dreamed of doing and be the things I've always wished to be. Instead of sitting and waiting for good things to come, I will stand up and create them. I will not lead a life of quiet resignation. Mine will be loud, bright, passionate, intense... a masterpiece.

———— ❧ ————

Twenty years from now you will be more disappointed by the things that you didn't do than by the ones you did. So throw off the bowlines. Sail away from the safe harbor. Catch the trade winds in your sails. Explore. Dream. Discover.

~ Mark Twain

This life is yours
Take the power
to choose what you want to do
and do it well
Take the power
to love what you want in life
and love it honestly
Take the power
to walk in the forest
and be a part of nature
Take the power
to control your own life
No one else can do it for you
Nothing is too good for you
You deserve the best
Take the power
to make your life
healthy
exciting
worthwhile
and very happy
Take the power
to reach for your dreams

~ Susan Polis Schutz

Promise Yourself to...

Cherish Each Day

— ❧ —

When I open my eyes each morning, it will not be with frustration or resentment. I will not hit the snooze button. I will put my feet on the ground and realize that I've been given a gift... another chance to live my life, do my best, and come one step closer to happiness. Every day, I will set goals and reach them. I'll have dreams and live them. I'll make wishes and make them come true. I will see each day as a new beginning... leading to the happiest ending of all.

— ❧ —

May you envision today as a gift and
   tomorrow as another.
May you add a meaningful page to the diary
   of each new day, and may you make
   "living happily ever after..."
   something that will really come true.

~ Collin McCarty

Awaken today and every day
with the gift of dreams,
the grace of a grateful heart,
and the capacity to look toward
the brighter side of things.
Rise each morning
filled with an enthusiastic purpose
that gives you joy,
for joy will give you wings.
Start each morning
with the pleasure of anticipation,
and always anticipate good things.

~ Vickie M. Worsham

Every day is a gift filled with memories, smiles, new events, and changes in your way of doing things. It marks another notch in the calendar of life and a growing understanding of yourself.

Celebrate each day with excitement. Travel more roads, taste more of life, and sample as many of the wonders of this world as you can.

~ Betsy Bertram

Promise Yourself to...

Do the Things You Love

———— ❧ ————

I will no longer push aside the things I want to do in order to make time for the things I need to do. Instead of letting the days pass by in a flurry of errands and work, I will carve out at least 30 minutes every day to do something just for me. It doesn't matter what it is ~ as long as it makes my heart smile. Some days, I might find more than half an hour. But I promise that no matter how busy my day may be, I will never give myself less.

———— ❧ ————

Find the things that most matter to you.
Make sure that your responsibilities
still leave you with
the time and freedom for
the people and activities
that provide your deepest satisfaction.

~ Garry LaFollette

*S*pend a portion of every day doing something you'd like to do ❧ Inspire a smile in your heart before each day is through ❧

~ Douglas Pagels

*G*et from life all that you desire and more. Feel free to do whatever you want and let that freedom soar.

~ debbie burton-peddle

*A*sk yourself what would make you happy. As soon as you have an answer, make some time to do it. Whether it's starting that new book you've been wanting to read or writing one of your own, give yourself time every day to do something you enjoy. It's your life. Don't let the rest of the world tell you how to live it.

~ Rachyl Taylor

Promise Yourself to...

Learn Something New

———— ❧ ————

Today I will experience something new. I will learn from the world around me: from the words I read, the sounds I hear, the touches I feel, and the faces I see. Even through the course of my daily tasks, I will try to search for a new perspective, lean toward understanding, and make the commonplace a wondrous place to be.

———— ❧ ————

Your whole life will be a learning and growing experience, whose extent can only be imagined. Life will be your classroom.

~ Donna Gephart

Be a constant learner who is open to new ideas and concepts. Be willing to try new things, go to new places, and keep adventure and fun a top priority.

~ Barbara Cage

There are so many opportunities right in front of your nose ~ chances to learn new things and meet new people. Look into taking classes at a local college or community recreation center. Explore a hobby you've always enjoyed, such as pottery or photography, or take up a sport like tennis or golf. These are great ways to meet interesting people and cultivate new relationships. After a long day of work or school, it may be hard to find the motivation to do these things, but once you get yourself into a pattern, you will look forward to this time to unwind.

~ Diane Mastromarino

Make Today
a Day for You

———————— ❧ ————————

Today, I will do whatever
my heart tells me to do.
I'll sleep in if I feel like resting,
or I'll wake up early and watch the sun rise.
I'll go for a walk if I want to get outside,
or I'll just lie back and relax.
I'll eat bananas or chocolate,
peanut butter or popcorn.
I'll read or write, sing or dance,
work or play.
It's up to me.
The rest of the world
will just have to wait.
Today is mine.
All mine.

———————— ❧ ————————

Take a personal day off from work or school and sleep in. Take a very long bath or shower and use up all the hot water. Fill up a bowl with your favorite ice cream, and relax on the couch and indulge. Rent a classic love story or read your favorite book. Do whatever you need to do to make your heart feel good.

~ Diane Mastromarino

Talk your own language
Express your own soul
You owe nothing to another
    only to yourself
Speak of your highest thoughts
Be all you held in your childhood dreams
Decide today who you wish to be
Expand your horizons
Go where your heart leads
And always give thanks
For the treasure that is life

~ Lynette Ann Lane

Give Thanks for All You Have

————— ❧ —————

Instead of worrying about the things I don't have, I will look at what I do have and realize that I am blessed. Throughout the course of every day, I will search for things to give thanks for. A smile from a stranger, a compliment from a friend, a blue sky, a green light... these are all reasons to give thanks. When night comes, I will write down five things I am grateful for. The next night, I will write down five more. The more I search for blessings, the more I will find. Keeping my eyes open will keep my heart full.

————— ❧ —————

The unthankful heart... discovers no mercies; but let the thankful heart sweep through the day and, as the magnet finds the iron, so it will find, in every hour, some heavenly blessing.

~ Henry Ward Beecher

Be full of awareness
    of the beauty around you.
Be full of gratitude
    for friends and family,
for the goodness you find in others,
for your health and all you're capable of.

       ~ Barbara Cage

*A*ppreciate the little things; stop to enjoy a sunset
or the smell of a flower. Look for the happiness and the
goodness in life, and your life will be happy and good, too.

       ~ Barbara Cage

*L*ook around you and be thankful.
Count your blessings.
Instead of rushing here and there,
take the time
to appreciate your surroundings.

       ~ Beth Fagan Quinn

Promise Yourself to...

Slow Down

————— ❧ —————

I will find a way in my everyday life to slow the world down and take away some of the pressures ~ moments when the demands of making a living take too much away from making a life. I will give myself time to smile and relax. To show how much I care. To share my love. To say what's in my heart and on my mind. To stop and reflect on my goals.

————— ❧ —————

Don't run through life so fast
that you forget not only where you've been
but also where you're going.
Life is not a race,
but a journey to be savored
each step of the way.

~ Nancye Sims

Life can be so hectic, leaving you with little choice
but to be swept up in the hustle and bustle that each
day brings. Make today special. Slow down for a while,
maybe even stop time... forget your responsibilities
and concentrate on your dreams.

~ Vincent Arcoleo

Promise yourself to slow down
and enjoy each moment as it comes.
Set your goals and priorities,
but allow room for special activities and surprises.
Be flexible enough to stop along life's busy road
and enjoy nature or conversation with a stranger.
Make time for family and friends
and the special things you enjoy.

~ Barbara Cage

Promise Yourself to...

Appreciate Your Friends and Family

———— ————

- I won't ever take my loved ones for granted.
- I will love with all my heart.
- I will give more than I take.
- I will have heart-to-heart talks and really communicate.
- I will appreciate all the little, special things.
- I will recognize that our time spent together is a treasure.
- I will cherish this blessing.
- What our time together lacks in quantity, I will make up for with quality.

———— ————

The most memorable times are those spent with loved ones and good friends. The warmest moments in life are those where you feel valued and can celebrate in the joy of sharing a connection with someone else. Nothing can compare to that. It is what enhances each one of our journeys.

~ Betsy Bertram

Friends and family are most important. During your most difficult moments and exciting triumphs, they stand beside you. Keep them with you always. They will make life's journey much more rich and rewarding, not to mention fun.

~ Donna Gephart

 Fill your life with the joy of friends and family. Each day, seek out the pleasures and deep rewards of love and friendship.

~ Garry LaFollette

Promise Yourself to...

Be a Better Friend

———————— ❧ ————————

I will take the time
to understand and appreciate my friends.
I will listen when they have something to say
and sympathize with them when
they are going through a bad time.
I will accept them
for who they are.
I will not take them for granted.
I will not be envious of their successes,
but glad to be a part of them.
I will not run away
when they are in trouble,
but stay by their side
for as long as they need me.
I will believe unconditionally in them
and encourage them in whatever they do.

———————— ❧ ————————

Being a friend means
always being concerned
and always wanting to help.
It means commitment for
  a lifetime ~
through the good and the bad,
through the happy and the sad.
Being a friend is a responsibility.
It means setting aside
  your own troubles and feelings
to take the time to listen.
It means helping whenever possible,
even if it's an inconvenience
  or a burden to you.
Being a friend requires strength,
  patience, and understanding.
But more than anything else,
  it requires love.

~ Jeanne Radke

Promise Yourself to...

Live Each Day with Love

——————— ✿ ———————

I will make affection and thoughtfulness regular, ongoing parts of my life. I will remember that a simple kindness goes a long way.
I will put others first whenever possible.
I will realize that love can take any situation and make it better.
Love is the greatest power in the world, and nothing can stop all the good it can do.
I will always make it a part of my life.

——————— ✿ ———————

A sense of love rebuilds the body, lengthens the life, brings inspiration, expands business, opens the way in a thousand directions, overcomes any obstacle.

~ Emmet Fox

Love can withstand anything.
It is sacrifice and tears,
laughter and hugs.
It is understanding and patience.
It is wanting only the best
for others
and wanting to help any time
there is a need.
It is respect
and unexpected kindness.

~ Barbara Cage

You will find as you look back upon your life that the moments when you have really lived are the moments when you have done things in the spirit of love.

~ Henry Drummond

Promise Yourself to...

Put Your Love into Words

———— ❧ ————

Too many days pass by when the words I most want to say remain unsaid. Starting today, every time I think about the people in my life who mean the most, I will take the time to let them know. I won't wait for special occasions to send cards, write letters, give compliments, or give thanks. I will take every chance I get.

———— ❧ ————

Sometimes things happen in our lives that cause us to stop and think about the things that really matter and the people who are really important. Today, take the opportunity to tell someone they are very important to you. Tell them how much strength you get from their support, how much comfort from their caring. Tell them they make a difference in your life that you are grateful for.

~ Denise Johnston

The greatest gift you can offer is simply to tell someone that they mean a great deal to you and that your relationship is a treasured gift. Offer to them the valuable gift of love that they have so generously given to you.

~ Brenda Neville

You could wait until someone's birthday to send flowers or a gift. You could wait until Christmas to tell them how much they mean to your life. You could look at all the holidays to see which one day would have the most meaning, which day would best express your love...

Or you can realize that your loved ones are special every day. Tell them how much you love them every time you get the chance. Only then will it come close to equaling the love they bring to your life.

~ Melissa Merriman

Promise Yourself to...

Enjoy Life

———— ❀ ————

I will remember to stay open to life's pleasures. I'll get out and do things and have fun. I'll keep my heart young and always make time to play. I'll make sure to smile every day. I'll do all I can to paint my world bright with laughter and joy.

———— ❀ ————

Live every day with a spring in your step, a light in the dark, a promise to guide you, and a song in your heart.

~ Donna Fargo

No man is a failure who is enjoying life.

~ William Feather

Make time for play. Think back on all the wonderful moments you've had, all the laughter and smiles. Know that many more moments of joy await you.

~ Donna Gephart

Create a life of joy.
Feel love from the people around you.
Share your deepest emotions.
Feel the sun on your face
    and the wind through your hair.
Live for each moment, and
    enjoy every gift life has to offer.

~ Shannon Hudson

Never lose the ability to feel
    with open arms
all the passion and joy that life
    holds for you.

~ Joan Benicken

Let Go of Your Worries

———— ❧ ————

Too many hours of too many days are wasted worrying about bills and bank account balances, time and deadlines, sleep, stress, work, life. Today I will realize that worrying about whatever difficulty I'm facing won't get me anywhere. I will unwind the nerves in my stomach and calm the nagging thoughts in my mind. I will take a deep breath and let it all go. If I catch myself worrying about something that doesn't matter, I'll stop worrying about it. If I catch myself worrying about something that _does_ matter, I'll stop worrying about it ~ and start trying to fix it.

———— ❧ ————

Worry a little bit every day and in a lifetime you will lose a couple of years. If something is wrong, fix it if you can. But train yourself not to worry. Worry never fixes anything.

~ Mary Hemingway

Nothing wastes more energy than worrying.
The longer one carries a problem,
   the heavier it gets.
Don't take things too seriously.
Live a life of serenity, not a life of regrets.

~ Douglas Pagels

Put your worry~cards
out on the table
and deal with them later.

~ Ashley Rice

You deserve a day where worries don't get in the way
of anything. A day where ~ even if some people are
insensitive or unkind, you're not going to mind because
the blessings in your life are far, far better than the
burdens. Don't let a single thing rain on your parade.

~ Douglas Pagels

Promise Yourself to...

Look on the Bright Side

———————— ❧ ————————

Today I can complain because the weather is rainy or I can be thankful that the grass is getting watered for free ❧ Today I can feel sad that I don't have more money or I can be glad that my finances encourage me to plan my purchases wisely and guide me away from waste ❧ Today I can grumble about my health or I can rejoice that I am alive ❧ Today I can lament over all that my parents didn't give me when I was growing up or I can feel grateful that they allowed me to be born ❧ Today I can cry because roses have thorns or I can celebrate that thorns have roses ❧ Today I can mourn my lack of friends or I can excitedly embark upon a quest to discover new relationships ❧ Today I can whine because I have to go to work or I can shout for joy because I have a job to go to ❧ Today I can complain because I have to go to school or I can eagerly open my mind and fill it with knowledge and adventure ❧ Today I can dejectedly murmur because I have housework to do or I can feel grateful for shelter for my mind, body, and soul ❧ Today stretches ahead of me, waiting to be shaped, and here I am, the sculptor who gets to do the shaping. What today will be like is up to me. And I shall decide what kind of day I shall have!

Author Unknown

———————— ————————

It is the way you look at your life
that makes all the difference.
Your life is a matter of perception;
you can search for sunshine behind clouds
or look for rain hiding in blue skies.

~ Deanna Beisser

Attitude works wonders on bad days. Whether it's seeing
the humor in a situation, making a change, or accepting
something, attitude is one of the greatest forces in life.
Always remember that you can control yours.

~ Barbara Cage

Begin each day by focusing
on all that is good,
and you'll be in a position
to handle whatever comes along.

~ Linda E. Knight

Find Joy in Every Day

———— ❧ ————

I will never forget that the story of my life is written by the things I do every day. I will remember that the little things mean so much. I will fill my life with happiness by filling every day with a little bit of joy.

———— ❧ ————

Make sure to laugh every day.
Make it a point to look at things
   with a child's wonder,
to absorb the sights and smells of everyday life
as though you have never
   witnessed them before.
Swim in the beauty of every moment.
Realize what a miracle each second,
each minute, each hour is.
Write your name in the sand.
Dream impossible dreams
and make them come true.

Paint your days with a hundred crazy colors.
Dance! Inspire others with your flying feet.
Count the stars at night.
Watch for fireflies.
Give yourself a bouquet for no reason.
Listen to the rain on the roof.
Take nothing for granted.
Eat dark chocolate, and lick the spoon!
Realize you are beautiful, valuable,
    and mysterious...
there is no one like you anywhere.
Hold someone's hand.
Watch a late movie.
Forgive. Let someone off the hook.
Give your whole heart.
Love ~ every moment you can.
Remember to live your life.
Tell people you love them.
Tell them again. Don't ever forget.
Pray for peace in this lifetime.
And remember, joy is contagious.

~ Shavawn M. Berry

Promise Yourself to...

Remember What Is
Most Important

———— ❖ ————

I will remember to live life and enjoy it. I will remember to make my days happy, to fill my life with love, to slow down and appreciate every moment. I will remember what is most important in life... and I will shape my world around it.

———— ❖ ————

Remember that reaching your destination is only part of living. Enjoying the journey is the other.

Remember that no one person in life can make you happy. True happiness comes from within.

Remember that words are very powerful, and they stay around forever ~ so always make sure that what you say counts.

Remember that true love is the most precious gift of all, and the most tender of all emotions. Be sure to give it out as much as possible.

Remember that no one has all the answers to life. Life is an adventure that must be enjoyed to the fullest. Sometimes it is the surprises along the way that make it all worthwhile.

Remember that if today seems dark, tomorrow will always be brighter. Sometimes we need to get lost in the darkness before we can fully appreciate the light on our path.

Remember to appreciate the moment you are in. When you live in the past or for the future, you miss everything in between, and you will have never truly lived.

Remember that change is a good thing. When you learn new things and take on new challenges, you expand your mind and become a better person for it.

Remember that if you love someone, tell them. Life is short and it moves very quickly. Loving someone openly gives purpose and meaning to your days.

Remember to stop and take a breath. Life is not a race to be won. The only way to enjoy all of it is one moment at a time.

~ Rebecca Finkelstein

Promise Yourself to...

Remember Your Promises

———— ❧ ————

I will hold my promises close to my heart and let them guide the way toward a better, brighter tomorrow. They will remind me of my potential, my dreams, and my possibilities. They will be the tools I use every day to create the life I've always dreamed of living.

———— ❧ ————

Promise yourself...

- *To have confidence: when things get tough, when you're overwhelmed, when you think of giving up*
- *To have patience: with your own trials and temptations, and with others*
- *To have an adjustable attitude: one that doesn't react, but responds with well-thought-out actions*
- *To look for excitement: new things to enjoy and learn and experience*
- *To live with love: pure, unconditional, and eternal*

~ *Barbara Cage*

$\mathcal{P}$romise you'll always remember what a special person you are ✦ Promise you'll hold on to your hopes and reach out for your stars ✦ Promise you'll live with happiness over the years and over the miles ✦ Promise you'll "remember when..." and you'll always "look forward to..." ✦ Promise you'll do the things you always wanted to do ✦ Promise you'll cherish your dreams as treasures you have kept ✦ Promise you'll enjoy life day by day and step by step ✦ Promise you'll always remember to live a life of love and joy ✦

~ Collin McCarty

ACKNOWLEDGMENTS

We gratefully acknowledge the permission granted by the following authors, publishers, and authors' representatives to reprint poems or excerpts from their publications.

Barbara Cage for "Be a constant learner," "Promise yourself to slow down," and "I will make affection and thoughtfulness...." Copyright © 2003 by Barbara Cage. All rights reserved.

Lynette Ann Lane for "Talk your own language." Copyright © 2003 by Lynette Ann Lane. All rights reserved.

Betsy Bertram for "The most memorable times are those...." Copyright © 2003 by Betsy Bertram. All rights reserved.

Melissa Merriman for "You could wait until someone's birthday...." Copyright © 2003 by Melissa Merriman. All rights reserved.

PrimaDonna Entertainment Corp. for "Live every day with a spring in your step..." by Donna Fargo. Copyright © 2003 by PrimaDonna Entertainment Corp. All rights reserved.

Deanna Beisser for "It is the way you look at your life...." Copyright © 2003 by Deanna Beisser. All rights reserved.

Shavawn M. Berry for "Make sure to laugh every day." Copyright © 2003 by Shavawn M. Berry. All rights reserved.

Rebecca Finkelstein for "Remember that reaching your destination...." Copyright © 2003 by Rebecca Finkelstein. All rights reserved.

Vickie M. Worsham for "Awaken today and every day...." Copyright © 2003 by Vickie M. Worsham. All rights reserved.

A careful effort has been made to trace the ownership of selections used in this anthology in order to obtain permission to reprint copyrighted material and give proper credit to the copyright owners. If any error or omission has occurred, it is completely inadvertent, and we would like to make corrections in future editions provided that written notification is made to the publisher:

SPS STUDIOS, INC., P.O. Box 4549, Boulder, Colorado 80306.